KNIGHTON

TREF-Y-CLAWDD

THE TOWN ON OFFA'S DYKE

MARY CADWALLADER

First published 1996

Published by Wooden Books Ltd.
The Walkmill, Cascob, Presteigne,
Powys, Wales LD8 2NT

British Library Cataloguing in Publication Data
Cadwallader, Mary, 1909-
Knighton, The Town on The Dyke
A CIP catalogue record for this book is
available from the British Library

ISBN 0 9525862 6 6

Photographs prepared by
Artisan Print, Presteigne

Printed in Great Britain by
Woolnough Bookbinding Ltd,
Irthingborough, Northants

KNIGHTON

OFFA'S DYKE
MADE
IN THE YEAR
(A. 757. D.)

Contents

Dedicated to the memory of
my brother Ken

Introduction

Left: Artist's view of Old Knighton c. 1830 by J. M. Ince, a Presteigne artist. The Old Church, dedicated to St. Lawrence (1756-1878), makes a good focal point. One may pick out the original vicarage in Church Lane, the Norton Arms Hotel & Malthouse, the George and Dragon and the Old House in Broad Street. The hay-makers in Bonfire Lane complete a picture of summer peace.

I have in my possesion two, almost identical, books containing photographs of Old Knighton; they were both published during the first decade of this century, possibly 1905, by two local stationers, Edward Oldbury and William Harris, probably in a spirit of friendly rivalry.

As a child these photographs fascinated me, more especially as some were sold individually and it was customary to find them framed, hanging on the walls in friends' houses. I was always particularly intrigued by those mounted on glass and framed in 'plush' velvet (mostly dark apple green or rich ruby red). I think these were called 'OPAL' in the advert in Oldbury's book.

It wasn't until the mid 1970's that I realised the historical significance of these photographs. During a series of W.E.A. winter lectures our tutor Robin Cain suggested a book on Knighton. To my knowledge only one small book existed. It was researched and written by William Hatfield, my mother's uncle, and published in 1947 (the year that William died) with the help of a local committee. Its price was 7/6; now out of print, it fetches £30 or £50.

With the possibility of a book in mind my brother Kenneth and I started collecting Knighton photographs from friends and relatives. We were fortunate to have access to two large family albums containing a collection of 'used' postcards showing events of interest from 1900 up to the Second World War. It became evident that these cards were used instead of writing letters, and made a strong bond in the family, where the younger members were away from home.

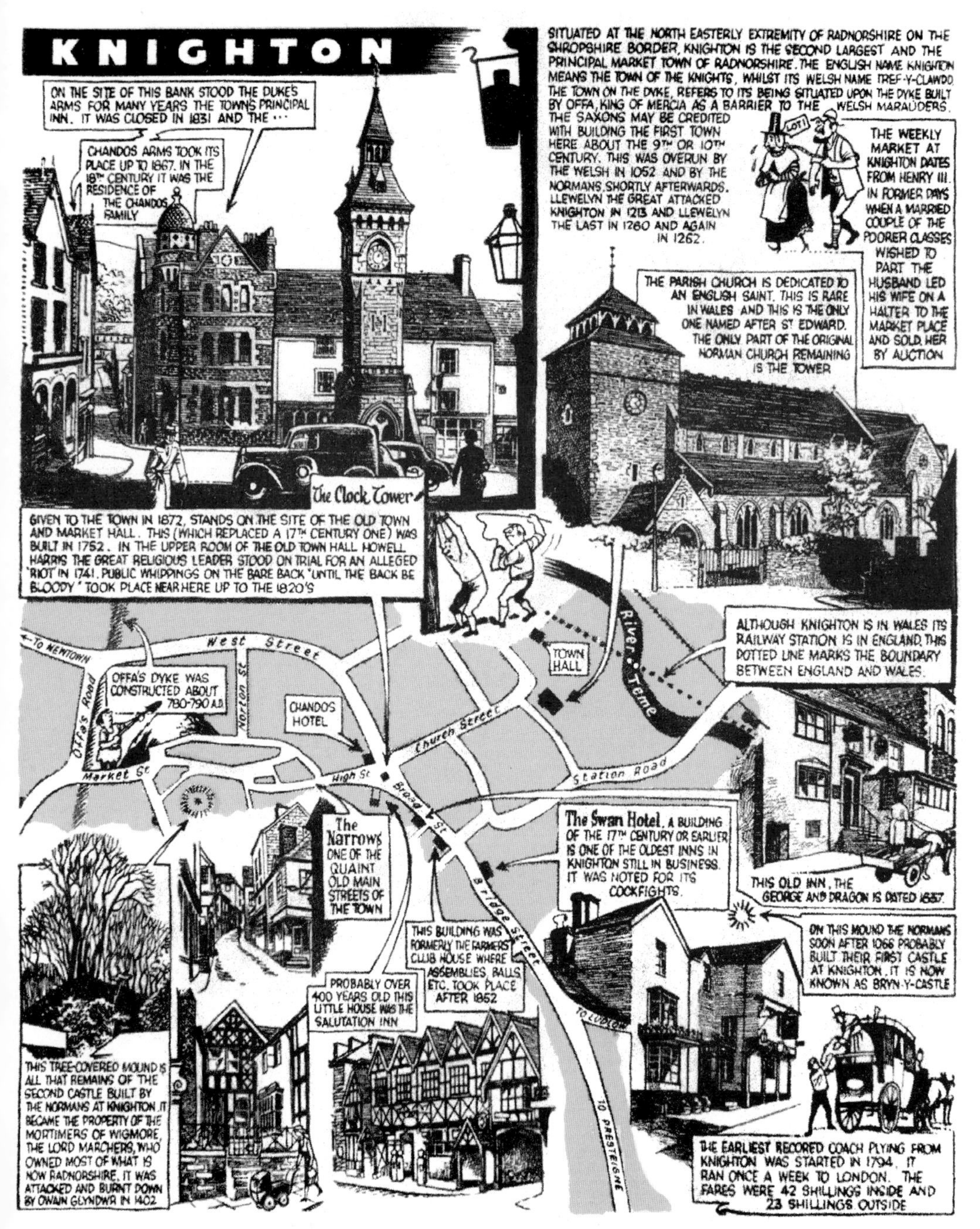

Left: A 'potted' history of Knighton by Geoffrey Evans of Evanjobb (by kind permission of the Editor of *The Western Mail*). It cleverly brings the past to life when Knighton was a market town, catering for its own needs and country folk alike.

I was able to borrow many postcards for copying and with the sponsorship of Tref-y-clawdd '1970' Society to stage an exhibition in the foyer of Knighton Library in the summer of 1981. Our local photographer Roger Bright undertook the copying of photographs, many of which were old and faded.

Four panels of school photographs, dating from 1890, are on show on the far wall of Knighton Library, together with others of interest. A further exhibition is now on show at the Offa's Dyke Centre in the Old Primary School, West Street - one school actually showing the class in the same classroom, 1928 - 29 (my class - Std IV).

Since the exhibition in 1981 so many kind friends have come forward with photos. May I take this opportunity to thank everyone for their help and encouragement. I hope they will forgive me if I do not mention individual names.

Below: South-west view of Knighton, Radnorshire. An old lithograph c. 1830 by E. Hodson. The old Church dedicated to St. Lawrence marks the site of Old Knighton, set against Kinsley Wood and Stowe Hill. Note the quarry sites on the hillsides.

Above: Knighton Town c. 1890. The Church (now dedicated to St. Edward) shows up well with its newly built nave, completed in 1878. The old small Chancel, still attached, was not rebuilt until 1896, funds having run out. It is interesting to locate the primitive Methodist Chapel in Broad Street, and the top of the Clock Tower, built in 1872.

My Town

At 86 years of age, born and bred in Knighton, I perhaps may be forgiven for describing it as "My Town". Situated as it is on the Border between England and Wales, it has had a violent history, with periods of utter devastation culminating in the sacking and burning of Knighton Castle by Owen Glyndawr in 1402, recovery from which must have been long and painful.

However, by 1540, 1585 and 1648, visiting historians were describing Knighton as "a praty Towne" - a pretty town it certainly was and it is likened to an Alpine town by William Hatfield in his book *Knighton* in 1947.

Left: Broad Street c. 1865. The lower building is The George and Dragon (1637), and above it an old house, probably of the same date and due for demolition in the 1880's. The George and Dragon still stands in 1996 and the building on the right was modernised and later became a shop and workshop.

Sadly, the face of Knighton has changed considerably during the last 25 years, and the Alpine picture is disappearing as housing estates climb steadily up the hillsides, and old footpaths are lost.

Fortunately, as long ago as 1230 Knighton was granted the right of holding a market every Thursday, and fairs lasting for three days around the feast of St. Matthew, 21st September. By the 1850's there were eight annual fairs, at which vast quantities of sheep and cattle were sold to buyers from many parts of England and Wales. In 1948 my Scholarship class (9 - 11 year olds) undertook the first 'pilot' project on 'Our Town', conducting a mini-census and showing by maps, charts, wall pictures and graphs just how Knighton as a market town served both town and countryside. It was a revelation to all of us. Today such a project would have shown up three faces of our town, namely Market, Industry and Tourism - in fact a changing face.

Right: A view down Broad Street showing The George and Dragon with its front extension in 1933.

Left: Broad Street. Shortly after 1896 Sidney Baker's shop was demolished and Clee & Sons built two imposing red brick, ground floor shops with accommod-ation above.

Clee's upper shop was known as 'London House', and was noted for its window displays of high class ladies' clothing. It had trained staff, a sempstress, a milliner and well appointed fitting rooms.

The lower shop sold bed-linen and general house-hold materials. A fascinat-ing glass show-case stood on the lower pavement, the children ranged in front of it obviously posing for their photographs.

The decorated poles suggest Queen Victoria's Diamond Jubilee Celebrations.

Left: Broad Street. 1896. Above the George and Dragon Sydney Baker has modernised his premises and produced a splendid display of goods when it was safe to leave them on show in the street. This photo is dated 15th June 1896. Obviously he wore his bowler hat on weekdays! His children look very Sunday best.

Names

Our town has two names (an English and a Welsh one), not surprising as Offa's Dyke runs through the west of the town - the old boundary between England and Wales.

The late Frank Noble relates the name Knighton to "Knight's Town" or *Chenistitune*, as it appears in the Domesday Book - there described as "was and is waste".

The Welsh name Tref-y-clawdd dates back to Rhodri Mawr, A.D. 840, some 50 years or so after the building of the Dyke by the Mercian King Offa. In translation "The Town on (or of) The Dyke".

Below: Broad Street. Mr. Davies the Malster, at the entrance to his Malthouse, an imposing building, extending from the butcher's shop to the Cwm entrance. Beyond this the Inn Sign shows "The George and Dragon", one of Knighton's oldest buildings, dated 1637. The Malthouse was demolished in the 1890's to make way for the Midland Bank, 1896.

Left: Church Street. c. 1880. On the left is the Chandos, the original town house of the Brydges family (later the Duke of Chandos). Note the imposing portico and railings. On the opposite corner W. J. Lewis had a draper's shop which later became the Birmingham and Counties Bank. On demolition Barclays Bank was built on the site in 1892.

Right: High Street. Continuing up the High Street we come to the Narrows, still decorated in Jubilee Mood. On the left Edward Oldbury's shop 'Grocer & Tea Dealer'. Across the street Solomon Baker's shop - a well-known confectionery and baker's shop. A family business, it was continued later by Charles Baker.

Shopping by Post in 1910

Mr. Charles Baker was our favourite baker in High Street. This is how his "Country Customers" communicated - with the help of a superb postal service.

Above: Broad Street. c. 1905. Left: Norton Arms Assembly Rooms with horse-drawn vehicle ready to collect visitors from the station or take the mail to Presteigne. Right: Mr. & Mrs. Harris' shop door-step. Two inn signs "George & Dragon" and "The Crown" face each other half way up the street.

Note: Postcard quoted on opposite page was posted 8 p.m. 8th August 1910. The bread was to be delivered by horse and van the next afternoon!

Note:
6d = sixpence (six penny worth),
of $^1/_2$ d (= halfpenny buns),
lbs = pounds.

From Betty Thomas' postcard showing Heyope Church, posted 8 p.m. August 8th 1910:

To Mr. Baker, Knighton Rads.

Please send 9 loaves of white bread tomorrow: as many tinned ones as possible - also 6d of ½ d buns.

I shall require 30 lbs of cake on Tuesday: 20 lbs of currant and 10 lbs plain.

Please quote price per driver tomorrow afternoon.

EL. J.

Below: The Tower Square and Church Street c. 1898. On the left The Old Post Office - note the letter box in window. The Old Post Office was converted into a shoe-shop by Gwyther & Son in 1922. E. Oldbury had a butcher's shop at Chandos, below.

Left: The Town Clock, built in 1872. William Hatfield writes, "In the centre of the town the most conspicuous object is the Clock Tower. Before 1872 the Old Town Hall stood on this site, the front facing Broad Street."

William's father saw it when he was young; there was much opposition to its removal. It was used as a Market Hall, an Assembly Room and the "Lock-Up" and Police Station occupied the basement.

The Clock Tower was given to the Town by Mr. Thomas Moore of Old Hall, Llanfihangel Rhydithon, a relative of William Hatfield's mother.

Right: The Old Post Office, High Street, before Gwyther & Son took over in 1921.

Post Master - Mr. Wedley.

Postmen (from left): Mr. W. Phillips, Mr. Stratford, Mr. R. Thomas (senior), Mr. Albert Powell, Mr. Chadd, Mr. Parker, Mr. C. Griffiths, Mr. Meyrick, ?, Mr. W. Hughes.

Counter staff: Mrs. Meyrick and three assistants.

Left: A "New Look" for the Old Post Office. James Gwyther at the door of his shoe-shop opened in 1922. Note "Old Post Office" above the doorway.

Right: A Wedding Dress? from Clee & Sons, London House, making dress 8/6. Signed by Mrs. A. E. Clee, August 1885.

HOUSE, BROAD ST, KNIGHTON 18

Mrs Griffiths

Bought of Clee & Sons,
Drapers and Milliners,
FAMILY MOURNING. Silk Mercers FUNERALS FURNISHED.
Robinsons Bristol
AND GENERAL WAREHOUSEMEN.

	£	s	d
11 yds Silk @ 3/6.	1	18	6
4 3/4 Alpaca @ 10½		4	2
3½ lining 5½		1	7½
Body & Sleeve lining 1/6		1	6
Butts & Twist 1/-		1	
6 lace @ 6½		[illegible]	2
Frilling 5½			5½
3½ Ribbon @ 8½		2	5½
Steel & Tape 6d			6
Silk, webbing, cotton &c 1/-		1	
Satin 3d			3
Making Dress 8/6.		8	6
	£ 3	3	3½

Recd with thanks
Aug 22 1885
A E Clee

Street Scenes and Family Shops

Left Top & Bottom: Two similar views of Broad Street c. 1905. A market day (Thursday) with goods on display at Clee's & Abley's (on left of photo). Two Inn signs - "The Crown" and "George and Dragon" below Clee's shop. The street leads on to Bridge Street where the Police Station is just visible.

Left: Broad Street - looking up towards the Clock Tower.

Left: Broad Street - looking down towards Bridge Street.

Right: Snow Scenes. The Clock Tower at night. On the left Meredith Thomas & Sons' draper's shop and The Old Post Office vacated in 1921.

Right: Church Street in snow. On the left The Chandos Hotel and David Davies' butcher's shop. On the right Barclays Bank.

Left: Station Road c. 1902 (formerly Tanner Street). Thatched cottage and "lean-to" shop owned by Mr. William Lowe, a dealer and supplier of fruit, vegetables etc., at the entrance to Station Bridge. Alongside, a coach-builder's premises. The boy with the hand-cart was a familiar figure in the early 1900's.

Right: Mr. Still, confectioner from Broad Street, on his "country round" deliveries.

Right: High Street. The India and China Tea Company stood on the steeply rising High Street, above Clee & Sons. On the doorstep Mr. Grainger, manager, Edmund Jones (Dutlas) and William Edwards (Horse & Jockey Inn), assistants. The errand boy, sporting a buttonhole, I cannot name. The photo is just previous to the 1st World War, possibly 1912.

Left: Broad Street c. 1912. A sunny August day - all the shop blinds are out! In the background the tents are set up for the Annual Show - the last Saturday in August. The street needs clearing up after Thursday's Market Day.

Right: Broad Street: Bradleys' - outfitter's shop decorated for Festival of Britain. It occupies the premises which was formerly W. A. Roberts' Hardware Shop and which is now Gwyther & Sons' Shoe Shop.

Right: C. F. Pugh's shop. c. 1930. A long established Ironmonger's Shop, formerly Meanley & Pugh, later Prince & Pugh, now incorporating Ironmonger's Shop with Clock Tower Restaurant.

Above: Broad Street. W. A. Roberts had an interesting hardware shop in Broad Street before the 1st World War. Described variously as Ironmonger, Implement Agent, Glass & China Dealer, he also displayed his goods safely on the pavement. Sadly he died during the war. Note - on the extreme right of the picture a board advertising "The White Star Line" shipping. It stands outside Mr. Still's confectionery shop. No doubt he was the agent for this shipping line.

Above: The Boxing Day Meet of the local fox-hounds at the Clock Tower c. late 1920's. In the back-ground The Old House (15th century?). An original Cruck House, it is one of Knighton's oldest buildings.

Left: A closer look at The Old House.

Left: High Street. Mrs. J. K. Goodwin kept King's Cafe in the High Street. She is pictured with her two sons and Flo Evans. Mrs. Goodwin was widowed during the 1st World War.

Left: Market Street. Hamar's Shop with interested neighbours, including Mr. Price, the Town Crier, complete with bell, ready to cry the latest news or inform the folk that the water was about to be cut off! On the left a butcher's shop owned by Mr. & Mrs. John Jones. This building is still standing; Hamar's and the cottages were demolished in the late 1960's to make room for a car park.

Right: Nelson Square. Edwin Stephens, his wife and two assistants at his Grocer's shop in Nelson Square (off Market Street). He later became assistant to Mr. Arthur Hamar.

Left: The Narrows. Mr. Bill Phillips surveying his array of whinberry baskets packed ready for the dealer to call and collect, or to be conveyed to Knighton Station for transport to the Midlands. In the window a selection of gramophone records - 78's. Inside a large poster advertising "His Master's Voice" records, complete with dog logo.

Left: A look down the narrows, c. 1900. On the left J. L. Allcock & Son, family grocers, and below Rees-Jones, draper with materials on display. Note Baker's horse ready for bread delivery. On the right Ernie Tudge, grocer, and below, other shops built under protruding jetties of the Old Salutation Inn (numbers 19-22 today).

Right: Photo taken further up the Narrows. Allcocks shop on the left facing William Lewis' bootshop with boots galore! The Narrows was a cobbled street, with a special drainage feature in the centre.

Above: The Top of the Narrows. Allcocks. c. 1890. How to display your goods in the "Good Old Days" (before the motor car). Mr. Allcock with son Charles, shop assistants and bakery staff. A family grocery of repute - now the site of the M. E. B. booster station.

Above: Market Street. Hamar's shop and warehouse c. 1932. Another family grocer of repute which served Knighton Town and particularly the Top of the Town and supplied country folk, firstly by horse-drawn vehicle, and then motorised (as picture). From left to right in the picture: Mr. Arthur Hamar, John James, Edwin Stephens, Bert Davies, Fred Parry, Jack Hamar (son), John Grimes, Fred Hamar (son), Lawton Stephens, Harry Steadman.

PUBLIC NOTICE:

NOTICE IS HEREBY GIVEN that all the Horses, Cattle, Donkeys, Sheep or other Animals found straying on any of the streets or public highways, within the Borough of KNIGHTON, will be impounded, and the fines imposed by the ACT of 5 & 6 William 4 C 56 will be strictly enforced.

Owners of Waggons, Carts, or other Conveyances who leave the same on any of such Streets or highways longer than is necessary for the loading or unloading of the same in any such street or highway, and all persons placing any manure, rubbish, or obstruction in or upon any or either of the same Streets or highways, will be summoned before the Magistrates and fined.

By order of the Local Board of Health for the Borough of Knighton.

Edward Weyman. SURVEYOR.

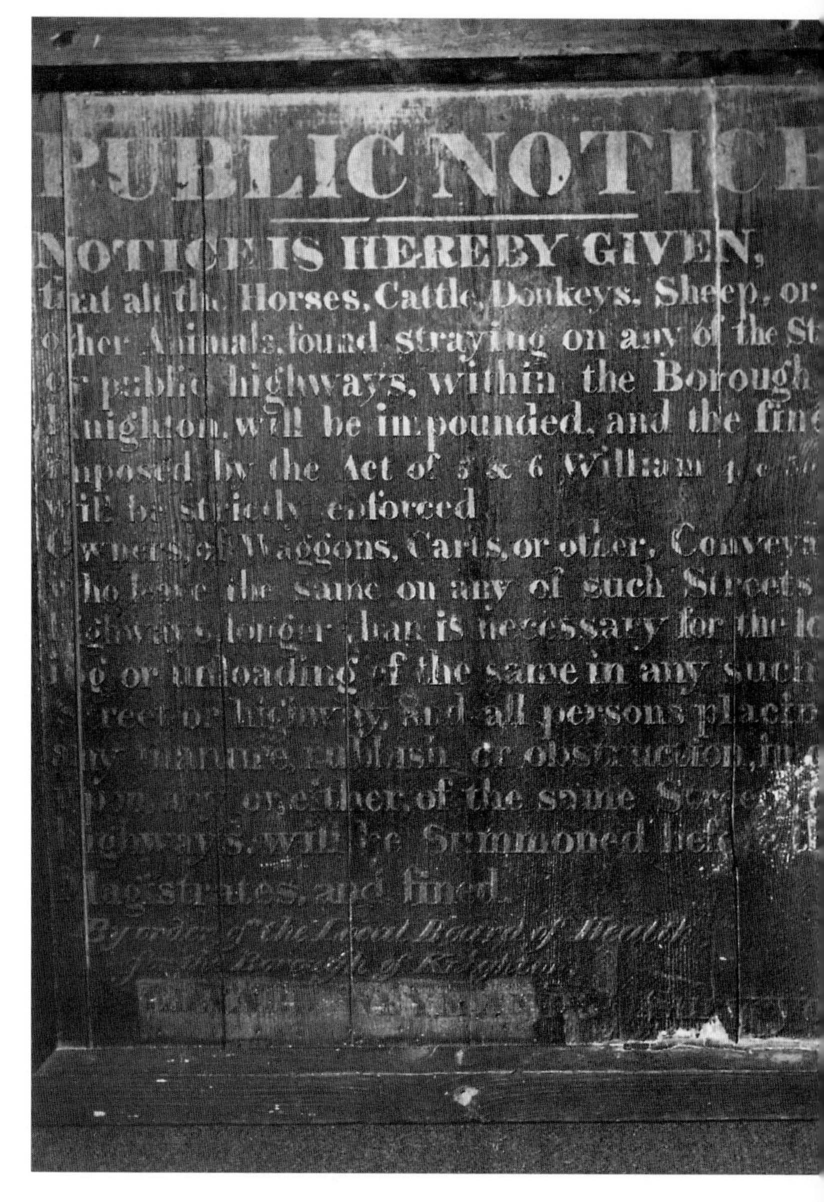

Above: Public Notice. c. 1853. This notice board was exhibited in West Street on the wall of the abattoir, near the Wesleyan Chapel. It concerns the impounding of stray animals and is signed by Edward Weyman, Surveyor, (it is now in the Museum at Llandrindod Wells). The Pound was in Almshouse St., now Wylcwm St.

West Street & Victoria Road

Right: A dangerous corner at the junction of High Street, Church Street, and West Street. By 1930, with the increase in motor traffic, it became necessary to demolish about one half of the Chandos in order to widen West Street.

Right: The Chandos - greatly reduced - almost ready for rebuilding. The carpenter on the roof is almost certainly the late George Roberts.

Right: West Street c. 1900. On the left Stephen Pugh's Caxton Printing Works and photography studio. On the right the Chandos, before partial demolition in 1931-32.

Left: Chandos, demolition in progress - workmen in precarious positions on roof in 1931. Notice on the left - "Teas Provided".

Left: The Chandos corner - widened in the summer of 1931, giving West Street a new look! Tom Williams (Woodhouse) plus two dogs awaiting the milk float.

Above: Before Victoria Road C. 1880. This photograph is taken from an open field in what became Victoria Road. Looking towards West Street it shows the newly built Wesleyan Chapel, and the Baptist Chapel (1865) on high ground known then as "Stars Close". Alongside, a bowling green and band-stand ran along the cemetery wall. Building commenced in Victoria Road in 1891 when William Hatfield built two villas at the junction of Church Street and Victoria Road, formerly called New Street.

Left: Victoria Road. The completed road after 1904 when the new Baptist Chapel was built to accommodate the Baptists who broke away from Norton Street Chapel (see gabled building on right- hand side).

Right: Victoria Road. Turning the corner one sees the first two houses on the left, "Ferndale" and "Willoughby", built by W. Cadwallader, my grandfather, in 1891-92.

Processions

Left: Coronation Day, Thursday June 22nd 1912. The children's Procession started from the National School, West Street. Mr. Perfect, Headmaster of the Boy's School, and Mrs. G. Perfect, Headmistress of the Infants' Dept. lead the procession. How I wish I might identify the children - I was two years old!

Written on the back of the photograph of the Coronation Day Procession (reproduced opposite) I found the following notes by E. E. Perfect:

"June 22nd 1912. This shows the front of our procession last Thursday. It was half a mile long. G and I are easily visible, but can you find Babs? She is in our girl's arms, looking over the wall, just above G's hat! It was quite a snapshot and we knew nothing about it till today when we saw this for sale."

"G" is Mrs. G. Perfect, "Babs" was her daughter, Mildred. This photograph was given to me by Mr. Perfect's son, the Reverend Leslie Perfect when he visited my exhibition of Knighton photographs in the foyer of Knighton library in 1981, seventy years after it was taken. It shows all the children of the National School on their way to Bryn-y-Castell for Coronation Day Celebrations. Mr. Perfect's notes on the reverse were a bonus!

Right: The "First after the War" procession of 1921. And what a crowd!

Right: Procession. c. 1905.
Band Master - Mr. Lewis.

Knighton's narrow, steep Broad Street was a wonderful place for processions, generally on their way to the Annual Flower Show on the last Saturday in August - led by a band, local or otherwise.

The band was always a major attraction, often Military Bands, which fascinated us as children. Occasionally it was a competitive occasion when bands played as they marched and judges were placed in upstairs rooms en route in order to assess for prizes.

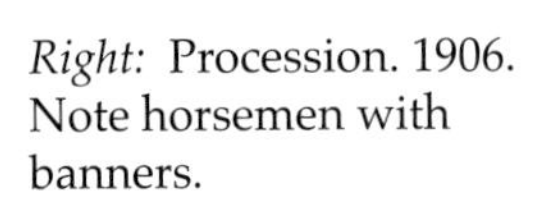

Right: Procession. 1906.
Note horsemen with banners.

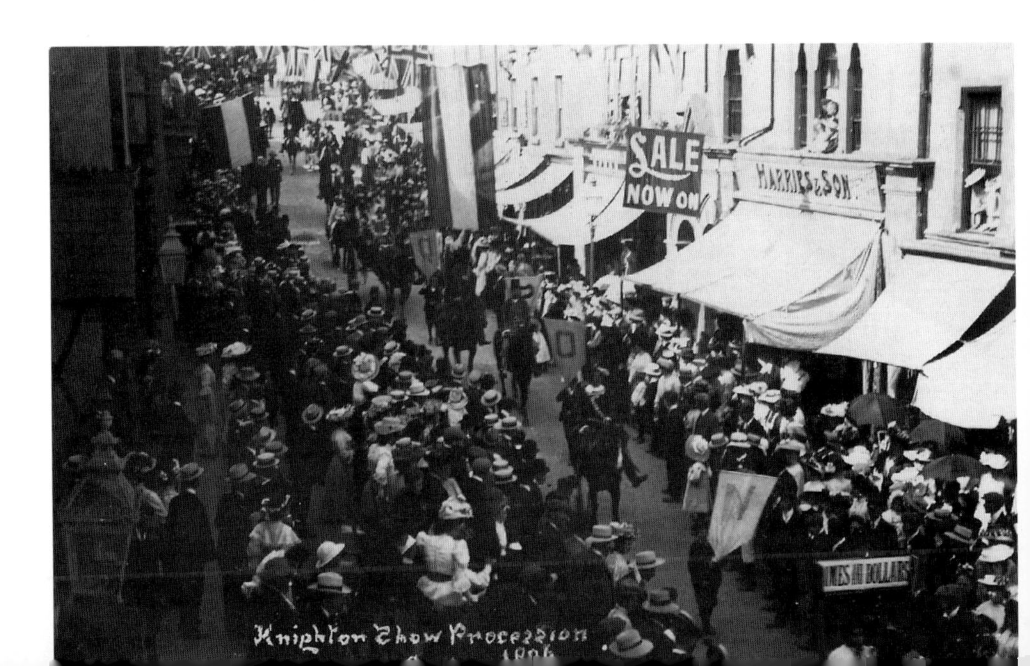

Right: Black Dyke Band passing Oldbury's Shop, on their way to Bryn-y-Castell, and the Flower Show, 1905. Playing to an appreciative crowd.

Right: A band in uniform, carrying a Horse Guards banner. Knighton Show, 1907.

Right: Show Procession before 1st. World War. Smocked volunteers appear to be pulling the antiquated fire engine, which later rested in the foyer of Knighton Library, West Street.

Right: The first show after the War, August 1921. Tom Norton's sign is now up at the Assembly Rooms and there is a vintage car on display.

Right: A Sunday School Outing c. 1905. Horse-drawn farm wagons preparing to take excited Sunday School children on their annual outing, probably to Brampton Bryan. Mrs. Morris and daughter Alice are on the steps of The Norton Arms Hotel, while Grandad Morris leads the fourth wagon.

Right: Knighton's own Band leading the 1921 procession. Jack Evans on coronet and Fred on drums.

KNIGHTON RAILWAY.

LINES WRITTEN ON THE OCCASION OF THE FIRST-SOD OF THE ABOVE RAILWAY BEING CUT

BY LADY JANE WALSH,

On the 19th of August, 1858.

Fill your bumpers, nine-times-nine,
Honour to the new fledged line,
Honour to the heads that planned,
Honour to the fair white hand
That, to-day, with keenest stroke,
Radnorshire's old soil hath broke.
Fill your bumpers, nine-times-nine,
Honour to the Knighton Line.

Honour to the jolly crew
Who combined the work to do:
Fill your bumpers, one cheer more,
Lo! from Cherbourgh's bristling shore,
With imperial honour crowned,
Brassey comes with fame renowned.
Fill your glasses! all combine,
Heart and hand, to speed the Line.

Here's to all his colleagues too,
Honour to the jolly crew;
Here's to Robertson, Maclean,
Here's to Field, and Peele and Green,
Not forgetting Charley Dean!
Fill your glasses! all combine,
Hearts and hands, to speed the Line.

The Coming of the Railway

Left: The Railway. The first sod cut. August 19th 1858. Poem by Lady Jane Walsh.

Thursday, 19th August 1858 was the great day for cutting the first sod on the line. The shopkeepers agreed to shut shop for the day - Market Day being Wednesday that week. Lady Jane Walsh, wife of Sir John, the M. P. for Radnorshire, was to have the honour. Not only did she cut the first sod, but she produced a poem, as did many others who burst into verse for the occasion.

The whole town was extravagantly decorated with banners galore, with such slogans as "Welcome" outside "The Cottage" (home of Richard Green, who became Sir Richard Green-Price) and "Radnorshire welcomes the Railway".

Right: The Teme Bridge. On approaching the Railway Station one crosses the Teme Bridge. In 1858 the River Teme was diverted from its course to accommodate the railway line, and a bridge was constructed. The photo shows the Teme Bridge in 1927 before it was strengthened and the roadway widened with pavements added.

Left: Knighton Station before the 1st World War. Well laid out and beautifully kept.

Luncheon was served in a marquee near the Chandos (probably where the Library is today) - "a cold collation" and wine to cost 5/- per person. Following lunch, music and dancing and later a "Variety of Rural Sports" (probably on the open ground opposite the Chandos, where Victoria Road would later be built).

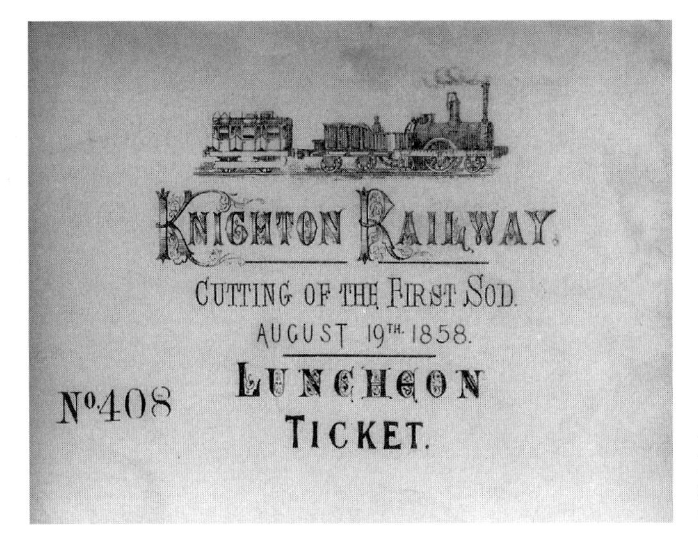
KNIGHTON RAILWAY.

CUTTING OF THE FIRST SOD.

AUGUST 19TH 1858.

No 408

LUNCHEON

TICKET.

Left: A Great Occasion. 500 people for lunch in a marquee opposite the Chandos.

At 11 o'clock a salute of cannon, a peal of bells and a procession of town's tradesmen and railway people moved off accompanied by two bands. The second band, the Shropshire Militia, were followed by four navvies carrying a mahogany wheelbarrow (which is still in the Museum at Llandrindod Wells), with the initials "K. R.", the town's coat of arms on the side - another navvy bearing a silver spade and two others bearing a model of the locomotive "Lady Jane".

Lady Jane cut the sod, placed the turf in the wheelbarrow which she wheeled up a small ramp to a low platform and tipped it over the side (presumably onto the proposed site for the line). Several dignitaries did likewise.

The procession re-formed and returned to the Chandos field - 500 people for luncheon, speeches and toasts. Needless to say all 'pubs' were full.

Note: It had been planned to open Knighton Station by May 1860, but weather in the winter of 1859-60 and a wet summer to follow delayed the opening until 6th March 1861.

Below: The picture on the left shows the old Teme Bridge, September 1927, before reconstruction. On the left the Central Wales Hotel; on the right gabled Station buildings & house and gasworks.
The picture on the right shows the New Bridge with widened roadway and pavements for added safety.

Left: H. R. H. The Prince of Wales on Knighton Station, summer 1926, on his way to Scout Rally at Llandrindod Wells. Guard of Honour - British Legion members.

Left: The Prince of Wales greeting Dr. Hunter, watched by Major Percy Rogers.

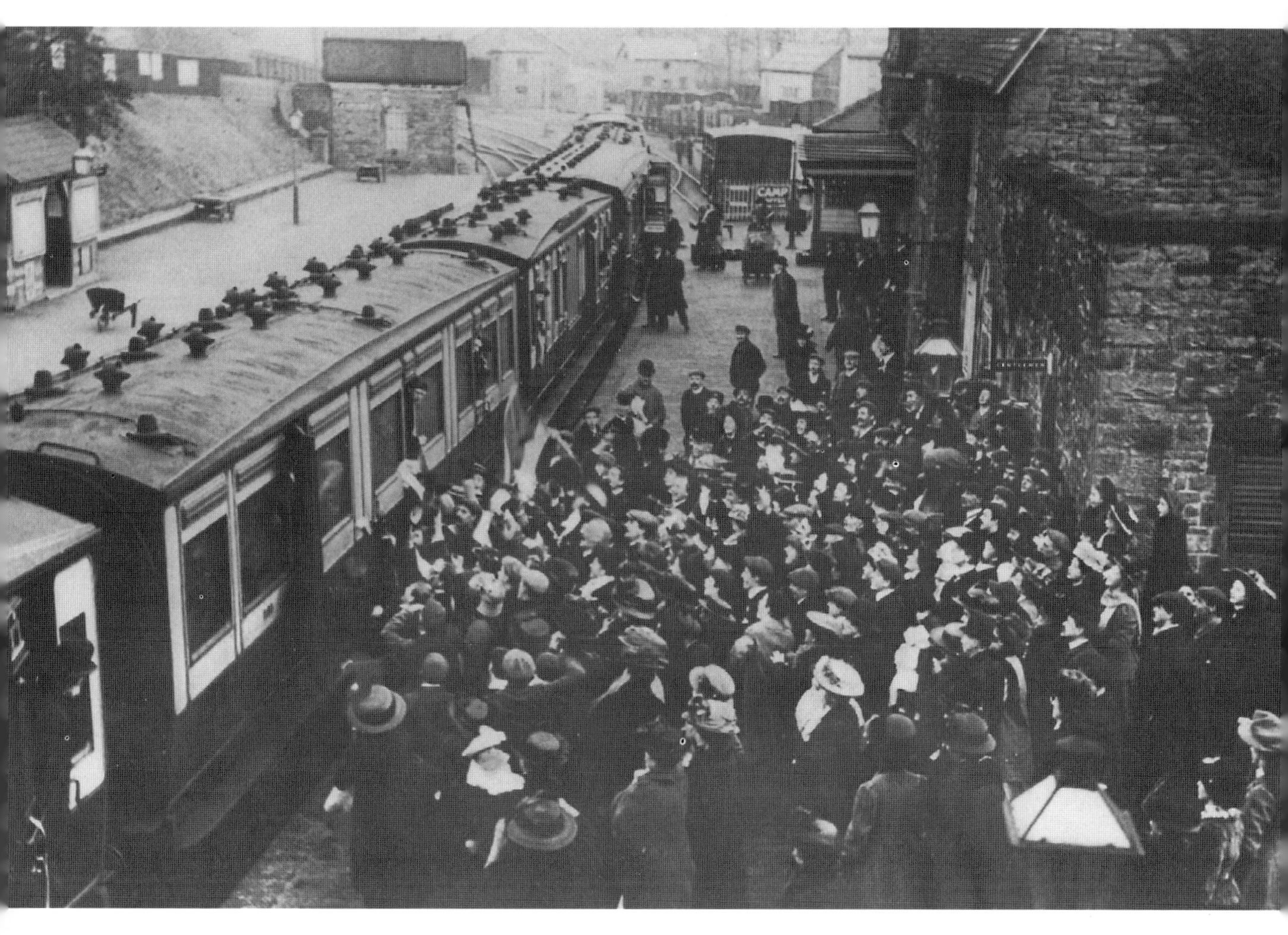

Above: Crowd scene on Knighton Station c. 1906. Possibly awaiting Lloyd George coming to attend the funeral of Sir Francis Edwards, judging by their dark clothing.

Right: Crowd scene on Knighton Station c. 1906.

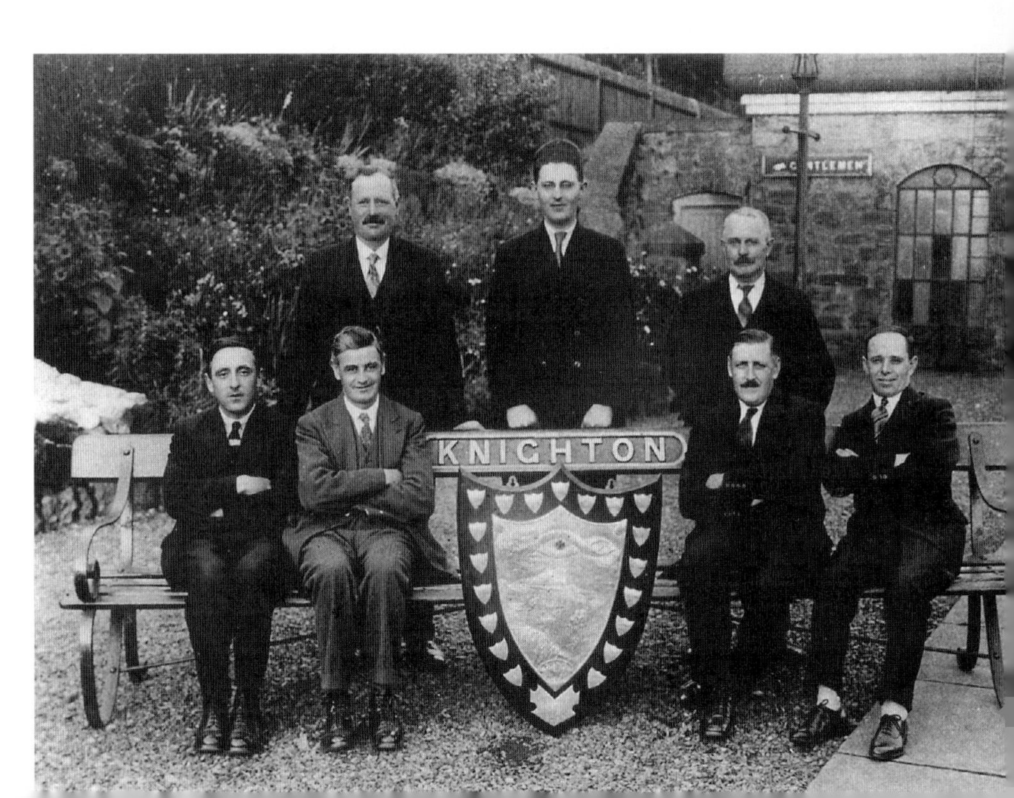

Right: Knighton Railwaymen win the Ambulance Shield.
Front Row: Cyril Lewis, Mr. Doug Taylor, Jim Lockett, Mr. E. Morgan.
Back Row: Mr. Hammond (Station Master), Oswald Davies and Mr. Watkins (Engine Driver).

Above: Knighton Station Staff in its Hey day! c 1925-30.

Top Row: T. Watts (Ganger), C. Hammond (Office), G. Cookson (Engine Driver), E. Wager (Guard), J. Evans (Fireman), ?.

Middle Row: H. Price (Porter), D. Taylor (Signalman), A. Taylor (Signalman), H. Hamar (Signalman), T. Evans (Foreman Ganger), G. Steventon (Linesman), B. Williams (Engine Driver), B. Powis (Ganger).

Front Row: T. Harding (porter), A. Powis (Booking Clerk), Mr. Shaw (Clerk), Mr. Hammond (Station Master), A. Smith (Clerk), J. Harvard (Signalman), T. Smallwood (Engine Driver).

And where are?: Mr. Samuel Preece (Engine Driver), Mr. William Watkins (Engine Driver), Mr. Elijah Jordan (Fireman), Mr. John Davies (Drayman), Mr. Richard Wellings (Porter), Mr. Passey (Porter), Mr. Jack Hamar (Fireman and Engine Driver), Mr. Evan Morgan, and perhaps others. I can only assume that they were on duty and not available for the photograph. Today we fight to keep our un-staffed station "open".

Right: Steam up at Knighton Station; trains from Swansea and Shrewsbury.

Below: Swansea train under bridge. Note the "Round house" above.

Left: Steam on our Railway Line! The Central Wales Express intrigued us as children - dashing by.

Left: Leisurely scene alongside the River Teme.

LMS

Left: John Davies, known as "John the Dray". The top picture taken at Knighton Station, ready to load up for town deliveries. On board John Davies, ?, Arthur Taylor (signalman) and Albert Powis (clerk).

Right: Children in Knighton Station Yard. Returning in bad weather, but still "Flying the Flag" (occasion not known).

Left: The day John Davies, Drayman, and his faithful horse retired. Isaac Marsh replaced the Horse and Dray with his Station Lorry. A sad day for John. On the left John and horse, on the right Isaac and lorry; in the centre the Station Master Mr. E. Parker and retired Station Master Mr. Hammond.

Memories of travelling the Line to Llandrindod Wells for 15 years:

A busy line:- used by school children, railway gangers, farmers' wives, to market, teachers, clerks, folk en route for spa treatment and by troops in both wars. Freight tains with heavy goods, fish trains, cattle and sheep trains before sheep lorries took over.

Right: Knighton Detachment of the 1st. Battalion Herefords Territorial Force, a few years before the 1st. World War.

Right: At Bryn-y-Castell, in 1911, the Knighton Detachment of the 1st. Battalion. Hereford's T. F. Probably on Church Parade. In 1914 most of these young men went to war.

War

On 4th August 1914 Belgium was invaded by Germany and at midnight England declared War. The following day, 5th August, Knighton's Territorials set off from Knighton Station.

Below: Knighton Territorials off to War. Knighton Station, August 5th 1914.

Right: A group of soldiers disembarking probably to spend a night at the Drill Hall before joining a regiment.

Below: "War". Knighton Territorials off to War. Knighton Station, August 5th 1914. Relatives and friends on "home" platform saying farewell to their loved ones.

Left: Knighton Workhouse - vacated at the outbreak of 1st. World War. It became the Red Cross Hospital under the supervision of Dr. Graves, and staffed by Mrs. Graves and V. A. D. nurses under Mrs. Coltman Rogers, their Commandant.

Right: 1st. World War cars meeting the Belgian wounded soldiers on their way to Knighton Red Cross Hospital. On the left Mr. Chadd saluting.

Left: Before War broke out. Knighton Football Team played Frankwell, St. George's, Salop in Church Stretton Charity Cup 1913-1914. Team: W. Evans, H. Griffiths, W. Stocking, L. Passant, A. Legge, W. Edwards, B. Jones, J. Evans, G. Roberts, J. Lloyd.

Right: Fancy Dress Football Match on Bryn-y-Castell, Christmas 1915, a respite from the War. Some players on Christmas leave before being posted to France; even Committee members dressed up!

Right: Another Football Team c. 1920's. Fresh young team after the War. Can you recognise Edgar Lewis, Gordon Tudge, Leslie Scutt, Victor Pugh and Hugh Jones? (Harold Griffiths now a member of the Committee).

Left: More fancy dress on Bryn-y-Castell. Folks keeping up their spirits in the 1st. World War years. William Evans, my Uncle, is the Pied Piper (extreme left).

Left: Belgian Soldiers at Knighton Red Cross Hospital, November 1914. The first casualties of the War.

Left: Dr. Graves with Belgian Officer and Mrs. Coltman Rogers' V. A. D. nursing staff, November 1914.

Above: Wounded Soldiers, local V. A. D. nurses.

Front Row - Miss Thomas and Miss D. Price with ?.

Second Row - Aggie Moore, Mrs C. Allcock, Mrs M. Machin, Hilda Hughes and Miss Edwards (Nant-y-groes).

Third Row - Miss F. Lewis, Miss Allcock, Miss Rogers (Stanage).

Left: A Knighton V. A. D. Garden Fete, and of course it rained!

Left: Dr. Graves with Belgian Officer and Mrs. Coltman Rogers' V. A. D. nursing staff, November 1914.

Left: Dr. Graves with Belgian Officer and Mrs. Coltman Rogers' V. A. D. nursing staff, November 1914.

Left: Dr. Graves with Belgian Officer and Mrs. Coltman Rogers' V. A. D. nursing staff, November 1914.

Left: The Crowd watching the Dedication Ceremony on 2nd October 1921.

Right: An Armistice Day Servive at the Cenotaph.

Left: Knighton War Memorial Dedication. 2nd October 1921.

Right: British Legion Members, photographed in Ystrad House grounds - survivors of the 1914-1918 War. The central figure is Major Percy Rogers. Richard (Dick) Thomas and I named almost all of them in 1989.

Left: Peace Day, July 19th 1919. A muster outside "The Plough Inn" at the Top of the Town - with local folk looking on.

Below: The Victory Tea - for wounded soldiers and local boys returned from the War - given by Miss Ethel Green at the Assembly Rooms.

Above: Miss Ethel Greene.

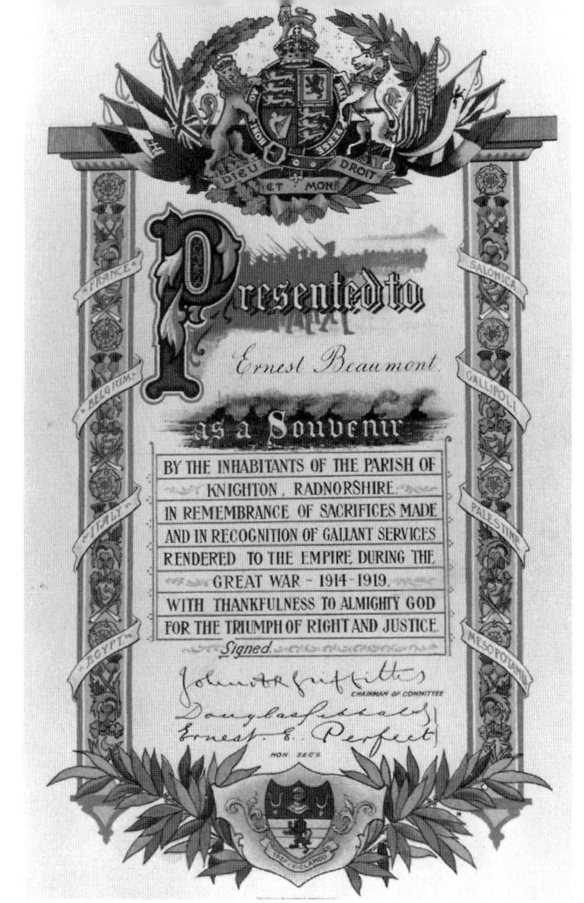

Presented to

Ernest Beaumont

as a Souvenir

BY THE INHABITANTS OF THE PARISH OF KNIGHTON, RADNORSHIRE. IN REMEMBRANCE OF SACRIFICES MADE AND IN RECOGNITION OF GALLANT SERVICES RENDERED TO THE EMPIRE DURING THE GREAT WAR - 1914-1919. WITH THANKFULNESS TO ALMIGHTY GOD FOR THE TRIUMPH OF RIGHT AND JUSTICE.

Signed.

CHAIRMAN OF COMMITTEE

Ernest E. Perfect

HON SEC'S

Above: Each soldier who returned received a Souvenir Presentation. Ernest Beaumont's name is on this one.

Left: Two local ladies ready to join the Peace Procession, 19th July 1919.

Left: Armistice Day at the Clock Tower, 11th November 1920. A small muster comprising anyone in the street when the clock struck eleven that morning. Lieut. Comm. H. J. Bragg in uniform, Jack Evans on the cornet.

Right: A crowd leaving the Drill Hall, 11th November 1922. Band and British Legion present.

Right: Peace Day Celebrations at Bryn-y-Castell.

Left: Peace Day Celebrations. Of course it rained but the band played on!

BRISTOL CITY

Knighton May Fair
17th & 18th May

Knighton May Fair was a time of great excitement for Knighton people as a whole, but especially for the children, who literally "had their ears to the ground" listening for the first engine's vibrations.

There were three sites for the fair:-

1. The Recreation Ground adjacent to the National School in West Street, which caused many headaches for the staff and resulted in one or two days holiday over May 17th (Fair Day) and often the 18th as well.

Marshall Hill with his wonderful traction engines, roundabouts and stalls held the largest fair in the Recreation Ground. He and his equipment came from Bedminster Down, Bristol, so it was not surprising that one of his engines was named "Bristol City".

His Fair was widely travelled, going as far afield as Olympia and Haverfordwest.

Left: One of Marshall Hill's wonderful traction engines, which came all the way from Bedminster, Bristol and was named "Bristol City". A source of interest to both adults and children.

2. The second Fair was staged in Nelson Square, off Market Street where Gotheimers set up their roundabout and stalls in the midst of the houses on the Top of the Town. One imagines the excitement of children in Nelson Square would be almost unbearable.

3. The third Fair was Farrell's which was set up in a field on Ffrydd Road, opposite the Workhouse, (later the Hospital). This field was often used as a Circus field when a menagerie came to town.

Right: A crowd at the May Fair early in this century.

Below: Mander's Sideshow with the Master and three maidens inviting their next audience. Some children were more interested in the photographer - especially the two in front.

Right: A small crowd in the Recreation Ground early in the century.

Left: Grand Hodgini's Circus - part of one May Fair scene c. 1910.

Above: May Fair. A packed Recreation Ground at the Fair before the 1st World War. A special time for country folk who flocked in from miles around.

Memories of Knighton May Fair
- by a Beguildy schoolboy of the 1880's

"When I was very young I went to Knighton May Fair. It was my first visit to the outside world...

"We were all excitement as the roofs of Knighton came into view, but before entering we had to pay the toll-gate keeper his fees for opening the gate. Our horse was stabled at the Red Lion, and we all went to a relation in the Narrows for lunch. I fail to remember much about the

Below: Runaway load in Broad Street c. 1911 or 1912. Marshall Hill's engine & loaded wagons coming down Broad Street, leaving Knighton Fair. The load, being too heavy on the steepest part of the street, ran amok and reversed the engine to face up street. One wagon finished up in Bradley's window. I understand that in future the wagons were taken down in order, first one, then two - the heaviest load being just behind the engine. The same applied uphill. The loads were re-assembled by the Old Police Station.

Fair, but to me it was a thousand times more wonderful than Felindre Wake. I do remember the cheapjacks near the big clock. One smashed a lot of dishes because people would not give him the price asked. I was told that this was a trick to draw a crowd. Another was selling dress goods...

"Then there was the ballad singer doing a good business, at the same time telling the crowd not to fold the ballads, which were printed on a tough kind of tissue paper, but crumple them up like a silk handkerchief and they would last a lifetime.

"Knighton seemed all "pubs" in those days, and they were filled to capacity from the faces I saw at every window upstairs and down. Quite often my mother and granny would stop and chat with relatives and friends, this being their annual meeting place. They kept a sharp hold on our hands to prevent us getting lost."

Knighton May Fair 1912

- by Nora Finch, a small girl from Stanage

Days leading up to the 17th of May find our little school at Stanage in a ferment of excitement. Anticipation of no other event in the year can cause such extremes of exhilaration and dismay.

Dismay because of the annual rumour that Marshall Hill has fallen out with Knighton Council, and will not be allowed to hold the Fair after all. An uneasy sense of reprieve when the rumour is contradicted, but we shall not be completely happy until the glorious day when the first steam traction engine comes chugging up the road drawing its mysterious covered trailer and caravan.

We rush in a body to the roadside, while speculation becomes rife and extremely wild. What particular attraction will this prove to be? The Circus? The Switchbacks? Surely that beautiful painted caravan with its gleaming brass must belong to the great Marshall Hill himself, on his way to crush the Knighton District Council, and proclaim the most stupendous Fair of all time?

We learn afterwards with awe that in fact a young member of the Hill family was born in Norton Street during one of the Fairs, and was actually christened "Knighton". What glory!

Excitement mounts as other engines appear in clouds of dust, accompanied by gipsy caravans and swarms of barefoot children, whom we regard with a certain

Left: May Fair Day at the Clock Tower c. 1905. Crowds and covered stalls. Note cobbled drainage channels.

Left: Street Scene from Chandos window. A peaceful scene where pedestrians might safely linger. Compare with 1996 when parked cars have taken over.

amount of envy - no school for them, and all the fun of the fair as long as it lasts! Our parents tell us that they remember roundabouts in Nelson's Square. In these days we are filled with resentment against the Knighton children. The fair is now held in their playground!

A school holiday will enable us to go on the second day, the first being considered unsuitable for children. Sensational rumours come back from the town - borne by questionable eye witnesses of serious breakdowns in Broad Street, and perilous diversions through Victoria Road. They have to be believed, as there are no other immediate means of communication.

In spite of all the misgivings and heartburnings the great day comes at last. We must be up at dawn to prepare for the three mile walk to the town from our house beyond Stanage. The old family perambulator is pressed into service, piled high with spare coats and other necessities, and destined to act as emergency transport should our small legs fail on us at the end of the day. We have eyes for the beauty of the May morning (was it always hot and dry?). All our thoughts are focussed on the thrills to come.

The roadside and hedges are completely blotted out by thick layers of dust; farmers' traps pass us in a continuous stream. There can be no question of getting a lift, every vehicle is filled to capacity. Carriers' carts convey the less fortunate from long distances. The more adventurous among us cling to the backs of traps, and are half dragged and half carried for a time, until arms can no longer stand the strain; then a luxurious pause on the hedge-bank to wait for the rest of the party.

Entering the town, we meet the full blast of music from the roundabout organs, played all day and most of the night without pause, and apparently accepted by the townspeople as one of the facts of life. The din is increased by the cries of encouragement from stall-holders and cheapjacks lining the streets.

Left: Knighton Show August 31st 1906.
Performing Dogs on show.

On the sweet stalls are piles of 'brandy snap' - seen at no other time - all happily exposed to the clouds of dust and swarms of flies. It looks delicious to us, but oddly enough we are discouraged from buying any.

Meanwhile, the farmers have 'put up' their horses and traps at the various hostelries, and notices appear in yards and gardens about the town, offering to take in bicycles at a charge of three pence. Amid scenes of utter confusion during the night, attempts will be made to reclaim the said bicycles, attended by furious arguments and drunken fights.

In the absence of any form of traffic, Broad Street is a solid mass of pedestrians all moving in one direction - towards the Fairground. Small girls like myself, in summer frocks, black-buttoned boots and the inevitable straw hat. No boy or girl is ever seen abroad without a hat. Women in long skirts and more hats, usually large and copiously trimmed with ribbon and flowers. Country men in dark Sunday suits, white collars chaffing unaccustomed necks. Young farm men making the most of their annual few days' holiday, the year's wages in their pockets, wearing the suits bought off the peg and donned on the spot in the clothier's shop. We are allowed a brief look round upon arrival, but are quickly hustled away to a meal at 'Mrs. Coopers' in Broad Street.

Long tables fitted into the confines of the small room. A collection of assorted humanity squeezed together upon the long benches. An attempt to cope with the cold meat upon a large plate, one's vision blocked by a gigantic cruet and the steamed-over panes of the little window. Flies zooming lazily overhead. Smells many and various overpowering, but at last the blessed release into the open air.

Entering the Fairground, we come upon the farm boys exhibiting their skill at the shooting galleries and coconut shies, watched by an audience of giggling young women, all bent on securing one of these opulent young men as an escort for the rest of the day. They will presently be seen, suitably paired, heading for a prolonged session on the roundabout, scarlet faced, bedecked with favours, coconut laden, triumphant.

The attractions are endless. Those magnificent girls in pink tights and frilly skirts, dancing on the platform outside the circus tent! The Wild Beast Show! Waxworks! The Boxing Booth - (we mustn't go in there). Hoop-la stalls with glittering prizes displayed on black velvet, and seemingly impossible to win; and over all the boom and crash of the music from the organs. 'Everybody's Doing It', 'Is London Like It Used to Be?' and 'Two Little Girls in Blue'.

Below: The German Aviator. Gustaf Hamel at Knighton Show 29th August 1913. He landed in "Eight Acre" field opposite and actually took passengers on short trips.

Some of us are too proud to patronise the junior roundabout, propelled by a man turning a handle. However, our legs are too short for greater things, and we long for the day when we too will ride nonchalantly round on those splendid galloping horses, cockerels, ostriches and other unlikely mounts. Until then we must be content with terrifying trips upon the switchback railway in the company of adults, two pennies for the fare clutched in sweating hands, waiting for the showman, who, amazingly, leaps from car to car while travelling at full speed.

'Swing Boats' are present, as also in the 'Cake-Walk', an invention which has gained fame locally from the fact that a very fat lady once became wedged in the narrow gangway, causing the mechanism to be stopped while she was rescued.

Another astounding novelty is the Ice Cream Man. Wearing a white coat, which doubtless proves the purity of his wares, he delves into a large metal box and produces surely the most rewarding of pennyworths! We have never seen it before, and we shall not see it again until next year.

The afternoon wears on, and noise, excitement, dust and exercise are taking their toll. We must begin to think of the long walk back home. Houses in Norton Street exhibit tempting signs such as 'Teas' but perhaps the funds are running low. We must take back some brandy snap and Knighton rock. A bottle of lemonade and some buns from Mr. Still's bakery in Broad Street will have to serve as refreshment; and having collected the perambulator, off we go.

The Fair is over, and we shall think of it for many days to come, but among the coats and bottles, the buns and coconuts in the old perambulator, for me, at last - oblivion.

Horse Drawn Floats.
Knighton Show c. 1905.

Right: 'Before & After'.

Bottom Right: 'Show Queen' & Attendants.

Above: The Ancient Frothblowers. Inspired by frequenters of The Horse and Jockey Inn. Jim Edwards and friends on their way to the Knighton Show.

Right: 'Fairyland'. c. 1905.

Right: Crowd leaving Bryn-y-Castell Show Ground - probably following a football match.

THE RADNORSHIRE
COAL, LIME & GENERAL SUPPLY C^OY L^IM
HEAD OFFICE:- KNIGHTON.

The Radnorshire Company

With the coming of the railway in 1861 Knighton was opened up to Shropshire, the Midlands and beyond.

The business men of Knighton saw the opportunity to form a trading company to bring in heavy goods like coal, building materials and fertilizers by rail. So in 1865 the "Radnorshire Coal, Lime and General Supply Company" came into being.

Depots were set up along the railway line from Broome to Llandrindod Wells and a "wharfsman" (salesman) put in charge. The main depot in Knighton was a substantial one, with an office in Broad Street, later in Wylcym Place. Later still a large-scaleSaw Mill was added near Knighton Station, and Animal Feeding stuff was manufactured. By 1961 an enlarged modernised Mill was opened with a brand new name to match - "RADCO".

The actual name of the business survived for 117 years. But after two take-overs it is now known as Dalgety.

eft: The Radnorshire Coal, ime and General Supply ompany Ltd. Head Office, nighton. An amusing hoto of what appears to be *small* company (see story n following pages). Mr. aron Wilding in charge vith Mr. Leslie Watts... eemingly awaiting the next rder!

Lucy's Story

It was 1923 when I arrived at the Radnorshire Coal, Lime and General Supplies Company's office to take up my new job, a very apprehensive 17 year old, remuneration £1 per week.

Entering through the heavy swing doors, with the frosted glass panels, inscribed with the "Radnorshire Co", I found myself in a large reception area, with an imposing wide staircase, with heavy mahogany banisters and a matching counter, where the cashier received payment for accounts and dealt with any day-to-day enquiries. At the end of one counter was a semi-enclosed area where he repaired to count his cash and do his sums preparatory to his daily visit to the Midland Bank. Between this and the inner office was a glass partition from floor to ceiling, behind which I was to spend the next 12 years.

Below: The Radnorshire Company. Men and trolleys in their yard alongside the Gasworks. Workmen: Jack Cadwallader, Leslie Watts and Aaron Wilding.

Above: Busy scenes at the Radnorshire Company's sawmills.

The main inner office was quite spacious, with two desks. One ran the whole length, behind it against the partition a smaller one. At the long desk sat four ledger clerks, - one of whom was me (the very junior clerk) - two men, and an older female clerk. The desks were sloping and very high with four high stools, hard, with oilcloth covered seats - one was not expected to be comfortable! One can imagine the kind of seat Bob Cratchett occupied.

The company's business operated throughout Radnorshire and just over the borders of Breconshire and Shropshire. There were a number of local depots throughout this agricultural area, and between the clerks we had 26 ledgers. So from 8.30 a.m. until 6.00 p.m. we had our noses to the grindstone, with 1 hour out for lunch. No tea or coffee breaks.

Often on our brief moments of conversation (mainly about something appertaining to the job) we were requested "to make less noise" by the secretary who reigned behind his glass partition, in his comfortable chair, and large flat desk. But we all accepted the rebuke without resentment, and were happy. This was the way of things in the 1920's.

Behind me, at the smaller desk, the Order Clerk and Office Boy pursued their work. The Office Boy addressed envelopes and ran errands. No-one else left the office unless they obtained permission.

Leading from the Main Office were the ladies' and gents' Cloakrooms. In a smaller side-office was the typist and filing cabinets. On the left, as you entered the front door, was the Managing Director's sanctum. We

always knew when he had arrived by the loud and prolonged sneezing to which he seemed prone. He was tall and lean and angular, with a very "Roman" nose. The Secretary was well-proportioned, bald and freckled - I think he had ginger hair. He would lean back in his chair, his thumbs stuck in the armholes of his waistcoat, listening to whatever one had to say, but never looked directly at you.

On the upper floor was the Boardroom - with a long polished table and high-backed chairs. This is where the Directors made major decisions for the Company. There was also a shelf-lined room where all the paper and office supplies were kept, and where the office boy took his comic, lying on the top shelf to read it! Many a time when the bosses went to get something they would go in and out without even knowing he was there! It would have been woebetide him if they had.

So the years passed. Very little changed, hard work and discipline seemed to be the keynote of our days. For instance, when we were doing the quarterly balance, after sending out hundreds of accounts, hand-written and itemized (the whole operation taking us about three weeks), we found overtime had to be worked to complete the job. We had to go back after tea for two or three hours; no extra pay for this, it was considered part of the job and was accepted as such.

In 1936 I left to get married and live in Birmingham, but was unknowingly to return in 1940 due to hostilities breaking out and the Company losing most of the staff to the War effort.

Birmingham was a vulnerable target for German bombers and no place for a young wife with a small son when her husband had been "called up".

Left: The Radnorshire Company. Photo of the timber yard behind the Company's Sawmills.

My grateful company allowed me 26/- per week Army Pay, on which I was expected to survive. I contacted the Army Pay Office but they said, as I had no Mortgage or debts (my rent was 20/6 per week), this was my total entitlement.

I was in a dilemma, but my problem was solved for me when the Company Secretary wrote asking me to return. My home was in Knighton. I put my furniture in store and returned to the Radnorshire Company for the duration of the War.

I found things much changed over these intervening years. Most of the men had gone to War and been replaced by female staff. There was even a cup of tea mid-morning.

Even the nature of the business had changed. Rationing had controlled the supplies of many commodities and often supplies had been included. The grain side of the business had been developed considerably, also building materials and artificial fertilizers. So my work was switched from Sales ledgers to the grain department, where not only seed grain was dealt with, but barley for malting for the large brewers was bought and sold. The paper room was coverted into my office and I had two typists.

I found this work very interesting, not so monotonous as book-keeping. In spite of the anxiety of War and the frugality of rationing, life in the Knighton countryside was very pleasant.

My husband returned in 1946. I again put away my books and set about making home once more - this time in my beloved Knighton.

Above: The Radnorshire Company's first fleet of lorries c. 1930. Workmen: Les Watts, Doug Trentham (office boy), Jack Cadwallader (chief mechanic), Alf Gill, Aaron Wilding, Glyn Jones. The small girl in the window is Doris Wilding.

THE GEORGE AND DRAGON INN
TO AVOID DISTURBING OUR
GUESTS WOULD COACHMEN AND
OSTLERS KINDLY REFRAIN
FROM SADDLING AND
HARNESSING BEFORE
SUNRISE
C.EYRE-LANDLORD
JANUARY 1853

Inns

According to Mr. W. H. Howse the names of 37 inns and public houses are known, which have been open in Knighton at some time or other since about 1750 - not all at the same time of course. There were, however, 22 in 1879 and even 16 in 1904.

It was interesting to note that the pubs seemed to be either alongside each other or in clusters - the Fleece, Seven Stars and King's Head facing each other on Market Square (the Top of the Town). The George and Dragon and The Crown faced each other in Broad Street, with The Bear, (in what is now The Old House) facing the Clock Tower. Another cluster was in Church Street - The Chandos, The Red Lion, The Duke's Arms.

At the bottom of the town The Norton Arms (1867), The Bridge Inn, The Talbot and The Swan.

Essential stabling for use on Thursday - market day, and particularly on fair and auction days, was available at all the inns. The Norton Arms, The Fleece and The George and Dragon, coaching inns, had special need for large stables, and an ostler to tend the horses.

Left: The George and Dragon Inn. "To avoid disturbing our customers, would coachmen and dealers kindly refrain from saddling and harnessing before sunrise." G. Eyre, Landlord, January 1853.

Behind the Crown Inn in Broad Street was a stable of considerable size, with a second storey and a corrugated iron roof. Known as the Iron Room it was used for dancing classes, socials, band practice and later for Scout meetings and other functions.

Inns were a feature of Knighton streets from Tudor times, notably the George and Dragon (1637), the Horse and Jockey and the Bear. The Salutation was an inn of considerable size, extending over three premises in the Narrows (numbers 19-21 today).

This inn had connections with the Chandos family and might well have housed some of their retainers. The frontage of the inn was jettied (overhung) and must have been quite imposing. Today's shop-fronts are added which rather spoils the historical feature. Only the Great Steps remain - the obvious entrance to the original Inn.

In the 19th century rather exclusive card and dancing Assemblies were held at the Assembly Rooms. Starting at 9 p.m. they lasted till day-break, supper being served in the middle of the proceedings.

The tickets were 5/- or 7/6 and one such function in 1864 had supper for 120 as follows:-

7 turkeys, 3 chines, 4 spare-ribs, 12 couple fowl, 3 brace pheasants, 2 brace partridge, 6 lobsters, 7 tongues, 3 pieces beef, 2 collared heads, Boar's head, 12 dishes hares, 2 galenies, 10 dishes of mince-pies, 10 dishes cheese cakes, tartlets, 4 dishes Dutch Flummery, 2 tipsy cakes, 2 dishes trifle, custards with exceptionally fine grapes, oranges, apples and other desert.

Not to mention the ususal "liberal supply" of champagne, wines etc.

In the 1920's the Assembly Rooms were still used for Socials and Dances. The New Year Ball was a favourite occasion, when the Norton Arms Hotel was open for cloaks and powder-room and one might sit out on the lovely stairs during the intervals.

Left: Interior of Norton Arms with imposing staircase, where we used to sit out when attending a Ball in the Assembly Rooms. Note: Hotel recently restored and changed to "Knighton Hotel".

Right: The Horse and Jockey Inn on the corner of Wylcwm Street c. 1925. One of Knighton's oldest buildings c. 1584. Still popular in 1996.

Left: The Norton Arms Hotel built by Sir Richard Green Price with Assembly Rooms attached, where Balls and Gala dinners were held.

Dec 6th 190 6.

Messrs F. Green & Nixon

TO W. W. TURNELL,

SWAN COMMERCIAL HOTEL

AND POSTING HOUSE.

KNIGHTON, RADNORSHIRE.

DEALER IN

WINES & SPIRITS

OF THE

FINEST QUALITY.

BUS MEETS ALL TRAINS.

		£	s	d
1906	Re Property Sale the Silurian Wool Mill			
Dec 6th	To Use of Room ordered by Messrs [illegible]		10	6
	Whisky, ale		6	6
		£	16	0

Left: The Swan Hotel. Dec 6th 1906. Bill for 10/6 for use of room when the Silurian Mill (on Mill Street) was sold to George Holroyd. Not forgetting whisky, 6/6.

Above: Fancy Dress Ball at the Assembly Rooms, Primrose Day, 1911. Many familiar faces including my father and mother in the foreground.

Knighton Market

Memories of the Market c. 1860, by an elderly Radnorshire Farmer from Llanfihangel Rhydithon.

"Knighton was the most convenient market for all farm produce. The large fair for livestock was in March when some of the best cart-horses and cobs were shown. The cattle were mostly stores - barren cows, young bullocks, and a very few fat cattle, but there were a few sheep at this time of the year.

Michaelmas Fair, on the first of October, was the great store ewe fair, when sheep taken from this parish left home as early as two or three o'clock in the morning. This was necessary as the buyers from a long distance came the night before; the market commencing soon after daylight. The same applied to the cattle fair on the second of October. This was the time when the big bullocks were shown. Some of the best were from The Farm, Bleddfa, The Moat, Beguildy and The Great House, Llangunllo."

.eft: First Sale by Auction at Knighton, on October 23rd 908. Good to have them off the streets.

Right: Broad Street at monthly fair c. 1905. Cattle and ponies still sold in the treets and "walked in". Sheep in pens behind the orton Arms Hotel.

Left: Sheep Auction at Knighton. Members of Knighton Urban District Council with visitors; Tudor Watkins (M.P.) with Rt. Hon. George Brown and Mr. Watkins of Radnorshire Company.

Left: The same day, with interested farmers Mr. Victor Pugh and onlooker, Mr. Stan Brisbane.

Councillors present: (from left to right) Morgan James, Ray Cuthbertson, Charles Masters (Chairman), William Roberts, Roy Waters, Howard Parker, Charles Cadwallader (my father), Clifford Richards (Clerk to K.U.D.C).

The Market Hall

The Market Hall (Town Hall), built in 1869, stood in Market Street in the high part of the town, above the Narrows.

The ground floor was a flourishing town market on Thursdays (market day) and on other special market days, especially the "Live Market" a week before Christmas, and "Dead Market" immediately before Christmas Day, when laden wagons laboured their way up steep Norton Street in very wintery weather.

The upper floor was used for many functions, among them the Quarter Sessions and early Assemblies. This large room had a stage where public concerts and entertainments were held.

Right: The Butter House. c. 1750 stood in Market Street on the square encircled by three inns - The Fleece, The King's Head and The Seven Stars.

Above: The much larger Butter Cross c. 1850 later stood on the same site as the Butter House. It was demolished, together with The Seven Stars, in 1869, to be replaced by a Market Hall. My grandmother lived at the Seven Stars until it was demolished. The Buttercross was sketched by my grandfather and drawn by me, based on her memories.

Travelling theatre companies came for a season and created much excitement, especially when for one week they performed "East Lynne", which involved children. These young actors attended our Primary School and were greatly admired.

Norton Street Baptist Chapel, not having a school-room, used the Town Hall for most of its functions - Harvest Suppers, sales, concerts and socials, at which competitive games were great fun.

The Amateur Gymnastics Club (c. 1905) trained there as did local choirs and bands. In later years the ground floor ceased to be a market and housed the Fire Engine, and became an egg-packing station during the 2nd World War.

During those years the upper floor became a Canteen for feeding our Primary School Children and the evacuees. Long lines of children from 4-5 years of age could be seen daily toiling up Norton Street for their "School dinners" - until 1970 when the school closed.

Subsequently the local Council took over the upper room for social functions and changed the name to the "Russell Rooms".

Demolition took place in 1987. *Note*: The Market Hall was built on the site of the old "Seven Stars" public house. Recently (1994) clearance work on the site revealed interesting arched cellars - obviously the wine cellars of the old "pub" which incidentally was being run by my Great Grandfather Thomas White when demolition took place, in order to build the Market Hall in 1869.

ight: The Market Hall, also alled the Town Hall, built y the Market Hall :ompany 1869, on the site f the Seven Stars Inn, on a pace of ground equal to ıat of the old Butter Cross. he photo shows the 1arket Hall ready for emolition in 1987. A very ıd sight to all "Old nightonians".

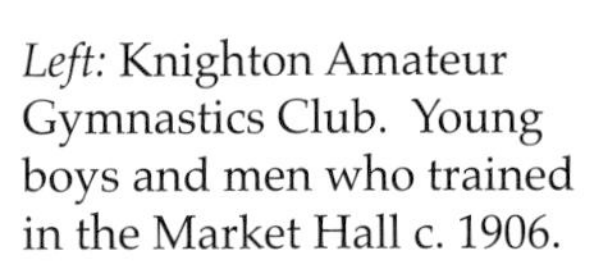

Left: Knighton Amateur Gymnastics Club. Young boys and men who trained in the Market Hall c. 1906.

Right: Demolition of the Old Police Station and Magistrate's Room, 1976. Another sad occasion!

Left: Looking down to North Toll-gate, Knucklas Road, from Conjuror's Pitch - the Tollhouse and gate just visible.

Toll-gates

There were toll gates on the five main roads leading into Knighton:

1. North Gate on Knucklas Road, at the bottom of Conjuror's Pitch.
2. West Gate on Penybont Road, where Frydd Road branches off.
3. South Gate on Presteigne Road near "The Grove".
4. East Gate at the Milebrook on the Ludlow Road.
5. On the Clun Road near "The Lea".

Toll-money was collected by the Toll-keeper on all vehicles and animals passing through the gates. This was used for the upkeep of the highway. Toll-gates were closed at 10 p.m.

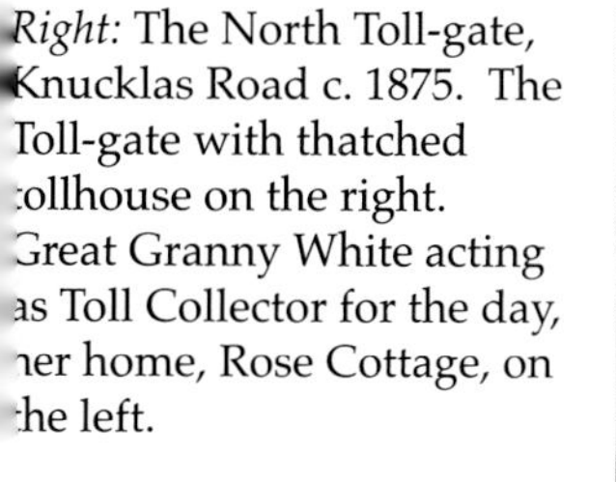

Right: The North Toll-gate, Knucklas Road c. 1875. The Toll-gate with thatched tollhouse on the right. Great Granny White acting as Toll Collector for the day, her home, Rose Cottage, on the left.

Above: Rose Cottage, Knucklas Road. Still thatched, but sadly in need of repair.

bove: Rose Cottage c. 1907.
t was demolished in the
930's - one of the last
hatched cottages.

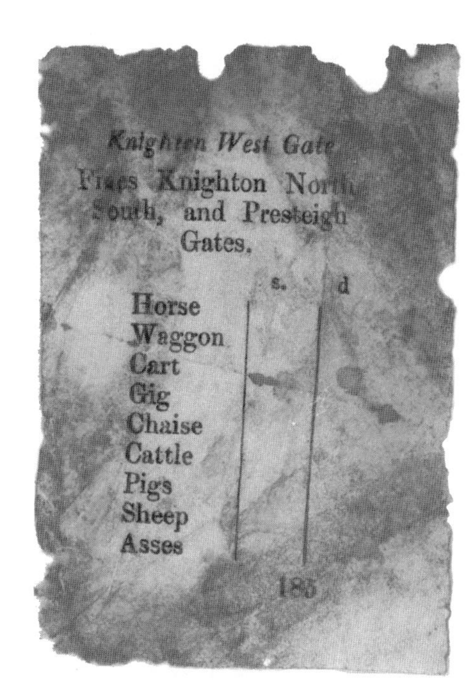

Knighton West Gate

Frees Knighton North
South, and Presteign
Gates.

	s.	d
Horse		
Waggon		
Cart		
Gig		
Chaise		
Cattle		
Pigs		
Sheep		
Asses		

185

Left: Toll-ticket for Knighton West Gate (Woodhouse toll-bar). This ticket frees Knighton North, South and Presteigne Gates.

Tolls:

Horse: 1 and a half pennies.
Waggon: 4d per horse.
Cart: 4d per horse.
Gig: 6d per horse.
Chase: 6d per horse.
Cattle: 10d per score.
Pigs: 5d per score.
Sheep: 5d per score
Asses: Half a penny.

Left: Serious Fire in Broad Street, December 6th 1911.

Floods, Fire and Explosion

ight: The Floods. October 0th, 1907. The River Teme as often in flood in utumn and Winter, wamping the pastures and ooding dwellings on Mill reen, Teme Green and tation Road. It had reviously been diverted hen the Railway Line was onstructed in 1858.

Glory day for old 'squirter'

One of Knighton's most remarkable treasures a very old fire engine, has just undergone restoration before being placed on exhibition in the local library. It is probably the oldest in Wales and among the oldest in Britain.

A similar model, which was said to have been manufactured between 1789 and 1820 was on show at the Fire Engine Exhibition at Crystal Palace 70 years ago, it was described as almost the oldest in existence.

Mounted in a heavy wooden box with iron-tyred wooden wheels and held in place by wooden uprights the old appliance is said to have been in use in Knighton between 1830 and 1850.

It was known as a "squirter" and is not to be confused with another appliance used in Knighton until 1920, the "manual", which was sold to Mr Davies of Buckwell for £5.

The apparatus consists of a tall metal cylinder into which water is pumped by way of dual pistons operated by side bars and then relayed through pipe and nozzle to the hose.

Water was pumped into the cylinder through a pipe inserted into a river or pond or even leather water buckets like one to be found at Bedstone School.

By 1880 the engine was housed in an outbuilding at the old workhouse, and was brought out occasionally for carnivals and shows as a curiosity. It ultimately passed into the possession of the former Knighton Urban District Council, though exactly when is unknown.

It was loaned for the Knighton and District Local History Exhibition in 1954 and at one time was in the museum of the Knighton Secondary Modern School. It was returned to the council when the museum was dismantled.

More information about this type of machine, which had to be hauled manually to a fire and required a crew of 16 to operate on the principle "eight on, eight off", have come to light as a result of investigation by veterinary surgeon Mr Lynn Lewis.

He has discovered that the Knighton machine was manufactured by John Bristol of Blaize Castle about 1780, and that there are only two other known examples of this engine, one in the Fire Brigade Museum at Morton-in-Marsh and the other in America.

He also discovered that engines of this type were used at the the Fire of London in 1666 but were not liked as they had to be hauled too close to a fire and often caught alight.

Until recently the engine has been in a bad state of repair but now it has been renovated and restored and the missing swivelling nozzle connecting the cylinder with the hose has been traced and replaced.

The woodwork too, has been restored instead of replaced which keeps the appliancea in its original condition.

Restoration has been a joint effort by local firms and individuals. J. Francis and Son, agricultural engineers of The Milebrook, Knighton, repaired the metalwork and stand; Les Wagstaff repaired and strengthened the chassis; a retired coppersmith, Harold Fletcher, repaired the cylinder; Robert Irving dismantled, cleaned and reassembled the metalwork; and Richards, the builders, provided labour and materials.

The project also had the encouragement and advice of two men who have since died... Jack Francis, the local blacksmith, and Jack Abams, the Chapel Lawn blacksmith.

With the woodwork repainted in the original green and with the metalwork cleaned up and polished, the engine looks very much as it must have done in its heyday. — **G.M — D.**

Above and Left: "The Old Squirter" Fire Engine was used in Knighton before 1880, then housed in outbuildings of the old Workhouse. It appeared later in Carnival procession and shows - restored by a dedicated team of Knighton craftsmen. Lately it has bee on show in the foyer of Knighton Library, but is now again in store due to alterations in the library.

:ight: The River Teme in
ood. October 1907.

ight: Gas explosion at
nighton Workhouse,
ecember 12th 1907. Sadly
e Workhouse Master was
lled. He had taken a
ndle when searching for
unpleasant smell. The
sult - a violent explosion
d loss of his life.

Above: Knighton Girl's School, 1937. Headmistress Mrs. A. M. Graves and her senior girls, two years before her retirement in 1939.

Knighton National Church School

The school was built in 1865 in West Street (then called Conjuror's Lane) on land donated by Sir Richard Green-Price. A purpose-built school, it was to take the place of a former school at The Great House, Bridge Street.

Built originally for 300 children, it had three departments, Boys, Girls and Infants, three headteachers and three front doors, facing the road. In the Summer holidays of 1911 a classroom was added on either end of the building by William Cadwallader (my grandfather) and their entrance doors then faced due West (Girls) and East (Boys).

The playground was comparatively small for over 300 children and playtimes had to be staggered until we obtained the use of the Recreation Ground - a field to the west of the building. This was also used for P. T. and Games.

elow: My Scholarship
Class. We had just had a
inging Lesson and
veryone was happy.
Ieadmaster Mr. Roy
Vaters. On top of the cup-
oard a baton, not a cane!

Above: Knighton Boys' School, 1937. Headmaster Mr. E. E. Perfect, with his senior boys, two years before his retirement. Some of these boys did not return from World War II.

In 1939 the three Head-teachers were due to retire and be replaced by one Headmaster to take over the whole school. So it was that Mrs. A. M. Graves, Headmistress of the Girls' School since 1906 and Mr. and Mrs. Perfect, Headteachers of the Boys' and Infants' since 1908 retired, and their place was taken by Mr. E. R. Waters, who combined the three schools. Long and devoted service was the pattern associated with Heads of Knighton National Primary School, each of the above teachers having

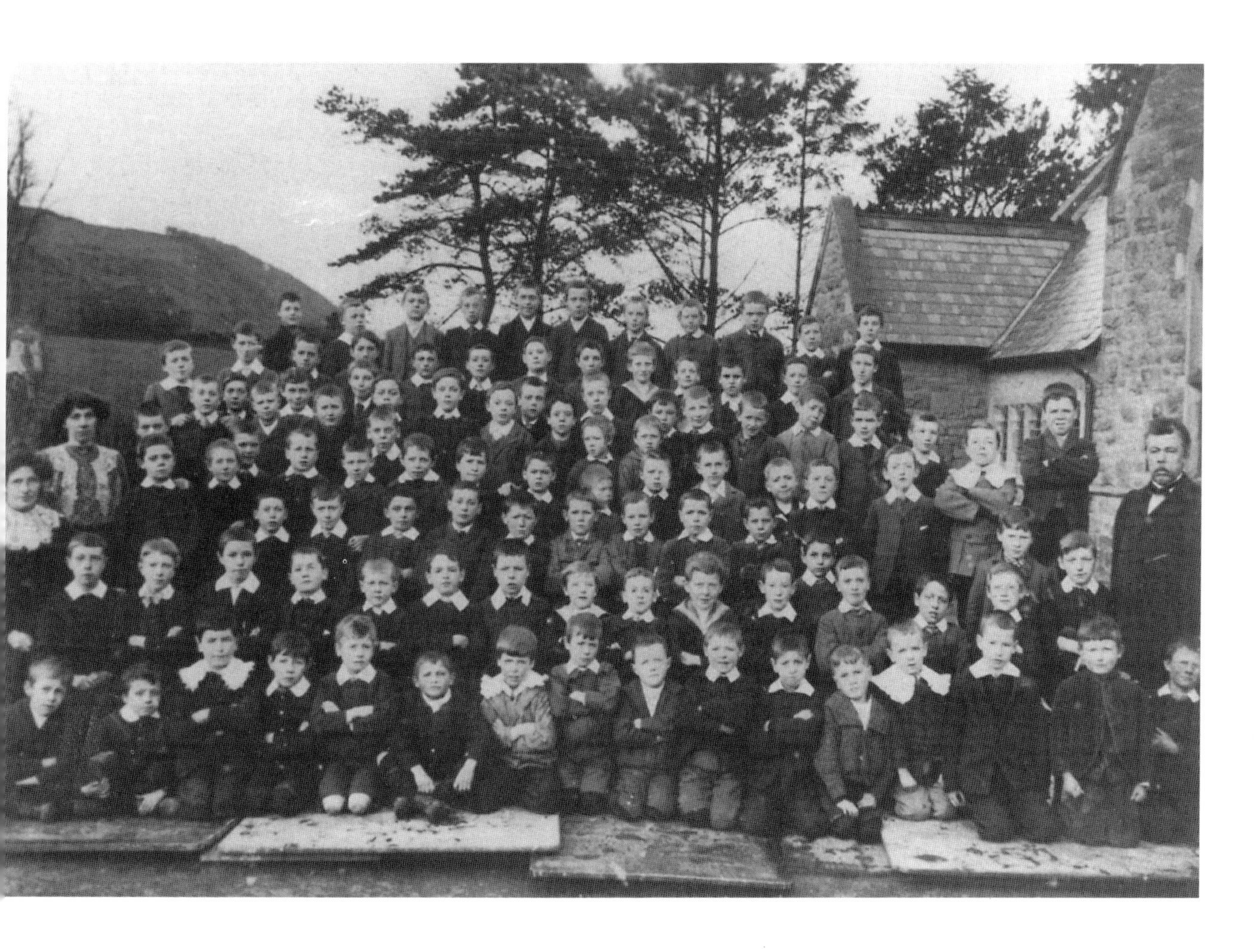

Above: Boys' School c. 1895. All the boys, balanced precariously on high desks. R. H. John Smyth, Headmaster, on the left two lady assistants. The boys appear to be wearing school uniform. I imagine they all went to the same tailor, probably Charles Evans, at Broad Street.

served for 30 years or more. This pattern was continued by Mr. Waters who served exactly 30 years.

I joined the staff in 1944, taking the place of two teachers (who had served during the war years) and served for 25 years.

Above: Infants' School. Mrs. Bessie Phillips and her "Babies" class c. 1923. A teacher dedicated to her Reception Class for many years.

ight: Bessie beside her
\ustin Seven" - F O 1833.

Knighton National Church School - September 1911

When the Schools open on September 5th there will be two additional class rooms! During the holiday Mr. William Cadwallader has been busily engaged in building on a classroom to the boys' and girls' department.

The old classroom will in each case be used as a cloak room, and the entrance will now be at the side of the building instead of the front. A good deal of the old playground has been taken for the new rooms, and so the Head Master's garden has of necessity been sacrificed to provide additional play ground.

The Foundation Managers have had some anxiety in finding the necessary sum of £500, but arrangements have now been made with the Bank, and with the consent of the National Society (who are trustees of the Ricketts Endowment) by which it has been possible to make this great improvement, without issuing an appeal, and of course without the cost coming on the rates, which would have been the case with a Council School.

It is probable that the formal opening of the new premises will not take place until a short time after the School has been open.

Left: Knighton National Church School (1865-1970). Playtime - a very congested playground with Infants' Headmistress on doorstep. c. 1898.

Right: Girls' School. Junior Class, complete with pinafores and supervised by big girl (monitress) on right.

Right: Girls' School c. 1895. Junior Class - more pinafores. Elegant teacher (on left) and monitress Emily Hatfield (on right). A favourite picture with 7 year-olds today.

The Church

Our Church is dedicated to St. Edward and is probably the fourth church on the site. There is a vague reference to a Saxon Church, circa 990 AD, and certainly a Norman Church around in 11th/12th century. The base of the Tower still retains Norman workmanship.

Like the town, the Church has had a chequered history. By 1752 the Norman Church was "in a parlous state, having been extensively propped and became a danger to the persons attending Divine Service", according to old records.

It was therefore demolished (except for the Tower), and a new church built, dedicated to St. Lawrence. Old pictures of its interior show a low, flat ceiling only 22 feet high, box pews and a three-decker pulpit. Also two galleries, one on the west (Tower) wall, built in 1770 and one on the north wall, added in 1816 to accommodate the vicar, his family and the parishioners.

In 1859 the new organ was placed in the west gallery where the choir sat. A small, low chancel completed the church dedicated to St. Lawrence.

By 1877 this church too was sadly in need of repair and the Victorians were busy rebuilding churches in the new style (Gothic). So again demolition took place and by 1878 the Nave was rebuilt as it appears today, lofty, light and airy: built at a cost of £3,750 mostly subscribed by parishioners and many friends who thought in terms of Grand Bazaars, and every conceivable way of raising money.

This dedication was to St. Edward; but it was not yet complete. Unfortunately, the chancel was not rebuilt until 1896-97, the money having run out, and for various reasons no more was forthcoming.

Left: The Church of St. Lawrence, 1753-1877. This church, built on open ground called Church Close, predates St. Edward's Church of 1878. One can just see the Churchyard wall and the lamp standard at the top of Church Lane.

It was nearly 20 years later, during the incumbency of Rev. M. A. Ricketts that the new chancel was built by my grandfather, William Cadwallader, with the co-operation of Messrs Weale and Elsmore.

The new Organ chamber was incorporated in the Chancel, and the organ was brought back from the Assembly Rooms where it had been stored.

Below: St. Edward's Church c. 1880. The new nave, built 1877-78 still has the old chancel attached. This was demolished and re-built 1896-97. The east window was then set up in the north aisle.

ight: At the Vicarage
arden Fete: an annual
vent before and after the
st World War. Mrs.
raves's girls entertain

ight: Vicarage Garden Fete.
nterested audience - Can
ou find Mr. & Mrs. J.
eaumont, Edgar Lewis and
Irs. W. Cadwallader?

Left: Vicarage Garden Fete. An annual event before anc after the 1st World War. Th C. E. M. S. craft stall.

Right: St. Edward's Church c. 1927 after the Church Hall was built.

ight: The Church of St. awrence, 1753-1877. Low nterior, decorated for hristmas, showing Organ n the West Gallery (1770); he North Gallery (1816); he three decker pulpit (left oreground) and Box Pews.

Left: St. Edward's Church. Interior after the new chancel was built - Note large East Window and original window in North Aisle. New stained-glass window on right. Top centre shows hanging corona with gas lighting.

Left: Bell Ringers at Knighton Vicarage with Rev. T. S. P. Griffith and Rev. Luther Thomas (curate).

Left: Churchmen returned from 1st World War. Sunday 1st March 1920, at the Vicarage.

Back row: J. Cartwright, R. Jordan, ?, H. Abley, S. Clee, H. Jones.

Front row: P. Pullen?, R. Thomas, W. Evans, F. Prince, B. Thomas, O. Jones, J. Thomas.

Right: St. Edward's Church Bells 1914. Six bells ready to go to Barwell of Birmingham to be tuned and reconditioned.

Right: Eight bells returned from Barwell's October 24th 1914. Two extra bells given by Mr. H. J. Bishop to complete the octave. The Rev. D. G. Macpherson, Churchmen and Workmen.

Above: Builders on the site, taking time off to be photographed. It is though to be the building of Knighton Workhouse, with the Master Builder, Mr. John Williams 4th from right on the slanting scaffold. Mr. Williams also built the Nave of St. Edwards Church 1878

Men at Work

Right: Three Knighton Families at Work.

Centre Front: Mr. Roberts and seated aloft, son William Roberts (carpenters). Behind Mr. Roberts is Edwin Evans (my Grandfather) and, standing (R.H.), his son William Evans (carpenters).

Standing: (L.H.) William Cadwallader and (R.H.) John Cadwallader (uncle and nephew, bricklayers).

Left: Birmingham Waterworks. Workers on the aqueduct at Knighton c. 1900-1910.

eft: Men at work in)wen's Yard. A good view f "The Round House" and :insley Terrace - former .ailway houses.

KNIGHTON, RADNORSHIRE.

Sale of FREEHOLD MILL PREMISES AND WOOLLEN MANUFACTURING PLANT.

GEO. TINKER & SON

Will offer for Sale by Auction,

AT THE SWAN HOTEL, KNIGHTON,

ON THURSDAY, DEC. 6th, 1906

At Four o'clock in the Afternoon, subject to such Conditions as will be then produced.

ALL THOSE

FREEHOLD MANUFACTURING PREMISES

CALLED

"SILURIAN MILLS"

Situate at Knighton, in the occupation of Mr. Thos. F. Wills, comprising--Three-storey Stone-built MILL, Two-storey BUILDING forming ENGINE HOUSE and WATER WHEEL HOUSE with STORES over, BOILER HOUSE, FINISHING SHED, DYE-HOUSE, Range of Two-storey Buildings used as WOOL STORES, OFFICES, and WAREHOUSE, together with WILLEY SHED, STABLES, Out-conveniences, and CLOSE OF LAND.

Situate at Knighton, in the occupation of Mr. Thos. F. Wills, comprising--Three-storey Stone-built MILL, Two-storey BUILDING forming ENGINE HOUSE and WATER WHEEL HOUSE with STORES over, BOILER HOUSE, FINISHING SHED, DYE-HOUSE, Range of Two-storey Buildings used as WOOL STORES, OFFICES, and WAREHOUSE, together with WILLEY SHED, STABLES, Out-conveniences, and CLOSE OF LAND.

The Motive Power comprises:--CYLINDRICAL STEAM BOILER, 20ft by 6ft. 6in. diameter with mountings and fittings; VERTICAL STEAM ENGINE, 12in. cylinder, 24in stroke; BREAST WATER WHEEL, 14ft. diameter, by 7ft. breast, with the Main Shafting, Gearing, Steam, Gas and Water Piping.

The site of the above premises contains an area of 1a. 1r. 5p. and is Freehold.

TOGETHER WITH THE

WOOLLEN MANUFACTURING PLANT

Upon the premises, comprising--Fearnought, Three Condenser Sets, Two pairs Self-acting Mules, Broad Beaming Frame, Two Warping Mills, Twisting Frame, Twenty-two Plain Flannel Looms, Washing Machine, Fulling Stock, Soap Boiling Pans, Squeezing Rollers, Whiteley's Patent Tentering Machine, Hydro Extractor, Hydraulic Press, Press Pump, Cast Iron Plate Oven, Measuring and Rolling Machine, Broad Raising Gig, Office Furnishings, &c., &c.

This offers a good opportunity to anyone to extend or open up a branch of the Woollen Industry, or the premises could be very readily adapted for the Yarn Trade or the Skin Hide and Wool Business, and there is an abundant Water Supply of excellent quality.

The Premises and Machinery will first be offered in one Lot; if not sold the Mill Premises will then be offered separately, and the Machinery sold out piecemeal by auction at a later date.

Further particulars may be had on application to the Auctioneers, at their Offices, 23, Market Street, Huddersfield; or to

F. L. GREEN & NIXSON,

SOLICITORS, KNIGHTON.

B. Brown & Son, Printers and Stationers, 23, Westgate, Huddersfield. Telephone 51X.

ight: Sale of the Silurian Iills. The Silurian Mills 'ere purchased by Mr. eorge Holroyd in 1906. Ir. Blackburn then came in 916 when Mr. Holroyd ined up for the 1st World /ar - and was later killed.

Left: "The Old Mill Wheel".

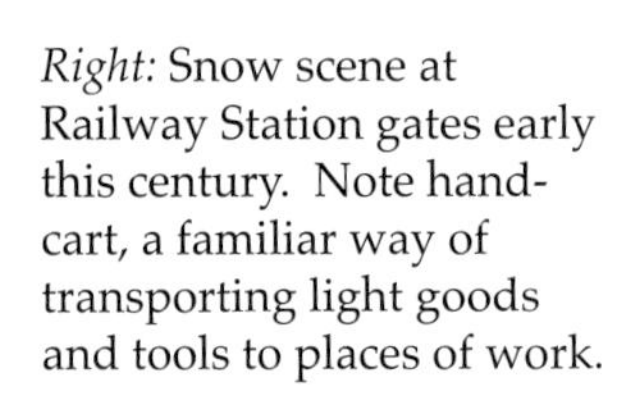

Right: Snow scene at Railway Station gates early this century. Note hand-cart, a familiar way of transporting light goods and tools to places of work.

Left: Mill Road, Knighton in the winter snow of 1906.

ight: Crabtree Walk
ading to the Riverside -
eautiful Chestnut tree
head - now felled for
ccess to Car Park.

Above: A sunny Sunday afternoon by the River Teme, c. 1905. A favourite spot for boys, just below Pinner's Hole.

Leisure and Entertainment

bove: "Under the Trees" - a
vourite walk into Kinsley
'ood c. 1920. Now much
ıanged.

Left: Scenes from "The Little Match Girl". Ann Thomas, Cissie Clee, Jessie Vaughan, Miriam Clee and, below, Nan Evans.

Right: Flo Evans and friends, including Vena Smith, Iris Seabourne, Sybil Griffiths, Mildred Perfect and Doris Evans.

ight: "Alice in Wonderland", y children of National chool, 'White Rabbit' - ucy Preece, 'Alice' - Mary loyd, 'Mad Hatter' - Stan udge. Card No.4 of earts - Mary Cadwallader. roducer Mrs. A. M. raves, Headmistress.

Left: At the Drill Hall, which was used by the Military, but was available (before the Church Hall was built) for Amateur Dramatics, Children's concerts, Whist drives and dances, Armistice Service and other gatherings - another Grand Concert has ended, date uncertain - possibly 1930's.

Above: Welsh Fayre. Knighton, 1936. W. I. ladies in Welsh costume. So many Knighton 'faces', how many can you recognise?

Left: Children's Section, girls in costume; boys in supporting role, not in costume.

bove: A charming group of
/eslyan ladies with an
xceedingly colourful
isplay. Entitled "The
ıpanese Bazaar" - held at
ıe Assembly Rooms 1911.
ostumes in figured muslin,
ıade by the Sewing Guild
ı Kimono style. Can you
ecognise Mrs. J. Beaumont,
Irs. A. Hamar, Mrs. E.
ldbury and other
Knighton" faces?

ght: Knighton Town Brass
ınd.

Above: Proclamation of King Edward VIII at Knighton on the steps of the Magistrates' Room, part of the Police Station (1937).

Front Row: Mr. Price (Griffin-Lloyd), Major Percy Rogers, Mr. C. Pugh, Mr. Pugh (The Grove)

Second Row: Sir Robert Green Price, Mr. Carless (Solicitor), Mr. Edwards (The Jockey Inn).

Back Row: Mr. Chadd (K. U. D. C. Councillor)

Elections and Proclamations

elow: Election Day. Frank dwards (later Sir Francis dwards) leaving Presteigne the County Town) for nighton, after being lected M. P. (His former ome at The Cottage is now home for the elderly).

Above: Tea Party at the Drill Hall. Probably given by Sir Francis Edwards for Liberal Ladies. He is seated at a table to the right of centre - bearded and elderly.

Left: Election result 1926 at Conservative Club, Broad Street. Capt. D'Arcy Hall meeting the townsfolk.

Right: Funeral Procession. Lloyd George and Mr. H. J. Clee at the burial of Sir Francis Edwards, 1927.

Right: A second procession in Broad Street.

GREAT
PROVISION
MARKET

Passive Resistance

In 1904 some local people refused to pay their portion of the Education Rate. Judging by the names quoted I recall they must have been nonconformists not wishing to be involved in what they considered a Church levy.

Apparently the equivalent levy was collected in "goods and chattels" and these were then sold at the Clock Tower. The auctioneer must have had a wondeful time disposing of such disparate articles as a sitting-room table, a silver cornet case, a silver lever watch, a bicycle, a tin of tea and two volumes of Greek Testament.

A Newspaper cutting from 1904 reads as follows:

PASSIVE RESISTERS' GOODS SEIZED AT KNIGHTON

On Friday the overseers of Knighton seized and stored away "goods and chattels" levied upon by distraint warrants for the recovery of the sectarian portion of the Education Rate.

Particulars of the amount and the articles seized are as follows:

Edwin H. Deacon, balance of Rate with costs, 8s 6d. - sitting-room table.
Rev. M. Amer, 5s 10 1/2 d. - two volumes Expositors Greek Testament.
Geo. H. Medlicott, 9s 6d. - silver cornet in case.
Rev. W. Williams, 6s 10 1/2 d. - silver lever watch.
Arthur H. Wainwright, 13s 7 1/2 d. - gold watch and chain.
Mrs. Stubbs, 7s 10d. - silver cake dish.
Edward J. Oldbury, 7s 10d. - eight-day clock and afternoon tea-table.
David Davies, Temperance Hotel, 9s 1d. - dozen silver-plated spoons, pair of carvers, and jam spoon and sugar tongs.
John G, Lloyd, 6s 6d. - silver lever watch.

Left: Passive Resisters' "Sale of the Century" at Knighton Clock Tower c. 1904. Interested crowd, probably looking for a bargain. Good view of Grocery Stores (later the site of the India and China Tea Company). Below the new imposing shops of Clee and Sons, and the George and Dragon Inn beyond the steps.

Arthur Owen, 10s. - lady's cycle.
David Milwyn Duggan, draper, 8s 6d. - pair of blankets.
James Anthony, 5s 10 $^{1}/_{2}$ d. - silver lever watch.
Wm. Weale, 5s 6d. - gold watch chain.
Wm. Hamar, 11s 7 $^{1}/_{2}$ d. - marble clock, two chairs and bellows.
Wm. Jordan, 5s 7d. - gent's cycle.
John L. Allcock, 13s 6d. - tin of tea, 12 ?? and two tins of biscuits.
James Heywood, 7s 9 $^{1}/_{2}$ d. - home-cured ham, 29 lbs.
Chas Jones, Upper Mill, 6s 10d. - silver lever watch.
Aaron Pugh, Grove Farm, 12s 6 $^{1}/_{2}$ d. - silver lever watch and chain.
Edward Parker, 6s 6d. - two watches.
Wm. Lewis, Overseer, 8s 5d. - two pairs gents' boots.

The Sale will probably be held on Friday or Saturday next. The authority to seize was included in one warrant only, and carried out by the overseers - a procedure that has considerably curtailed expenses.